A TRUE BOOK™

My United States

Arizona

JOSH GREGORY

Children's Press®
An Imprint of Scholastic Inc.

Content Consultant
James Wolfinger, PhD, Associate Dean and Professor
College of Education, DePaul University, Chicago, Illinois

Library of Congress Cataloging-in-Publication Data
Names: Gregory, Josh, author.
Title: Arizona / by Josh Gregory.
Description: New York, NY : Children's Press, an imprint of Scholastic Inc., 2018. | Series: A true book | Includes
    bibliographical references and index.
Identifiers: LCCN 2017048980 | ISBN 9780531235553 (library binding) | ISBN 9780531250730 (pbk.)
Subjects: LCSH: Arizona—Juvenile literature.
Classification: LCC F811.3 .G73 2017 | DDC 979.1—dc23
LC record available at https://lccn.loc.gov/2017048980

Photographs ©: cover: Michael Weber/imageBROKER/Aurora Photos; back cover: Nano Calvo/age fotostock; back cover ribbon: AliceLiddelle/Getty Images; 3 bottom: imageBROKER/Alamy Stock Photo; 3 map: Jim McMahon/Mapman ®; 4 bottom: Reid Dalland/ Shutterstock; 4 center: Rick & Nora Bowers/Alamy Stock Photo; 5 top: Kennan Harvey/Aurora Photos; 5 bottom: Alan Murphy/Minden Pictures; 7 top: LOOK Die Bildagentur der Fotografen GmbH/Alamy Stock Photo; 7 center top: Greg Vaughn/Alamy Stock Photo; 7 center bottom: Mark Newman/Getty Images; 7 bottom: Scott Warren/Aurora Photos; 8-9: DEA/Pubbli Aer Foto/Getty Images; 11: John Burcham/ Getty Images; 12: Kennan Harvey/Aurora Photos; 13: gary corbett/Alamy Stock Photo; 14: Morey Milbradt/Alamy Stock Photo; 15: Tom Vezo/Minden Pictures; 16-17: Nikreates/Alamy Stock Photo; 19: Kevin Fleming/Corbis/VCG/Getty Images; 20: Tigatelu/Dreamstime; 22 left: YAY Media AS/Alamy Stock Photo; 22 right: Pakmor/Shutterstock; 23 center: Reid Dalland/Shutterstock; 23 center right: Alan Murphy/ Minden Pictures; 23 top: Francois Gohier/Pantheon/Superstock, Inc.; 23 bottom right: Phil Degginger/Alamy Stock Photo; 23 center left: Igor Sokalski/Dreamstime; 23 bottom left: Rick & Nora Bowers/Alamy Stock Photo; 24-25: Education Images/Getty Images; 27: John Cancalosi/Alamy Stock Photo; 29: Saturated/Getty Images; 30 top: The Granger Collection; 30 bottom: Everett Collection/Superstock, Inc.; 31 top left: MPI/Getty Images; 31 top right: Bettmann/Getty Images; 31 bottom right: Mark Ralston/Getty Images; 31 bottom left: YAY Media AS/Alamy Stock Photo; 32: Underwood Archives/The Image Works; 33: Charles Ommanney/Getty Images; 34-35: Pat Canova/Getty Images; 36: Icon Sportswire/Getty Images; 37: Don Emmert/Getty Images; 38: Jim West/Alamy Stock Photo; 39: Bloomberg/Getty Images; 40 bottom right: Claudia Totir/Getty Images; 40 notebook: PepitoPhotos/Getty Images; 41: MakenaStockMedia/Pacific Stock-Design Pics/ Superstock, Inc.; 42 bottom left: Michael Ochs Archives/Getty Images; 42 top: Arthur Schatz/Getty Images; 42 bottom center: ZUMA Press, Inc./Alamy Stock Photo; 42 bottom right: Jaguar/Alamy Stock Photo; 43 top left: PA Images/Alamy Stock Photo; 43 top right: Splash News/ Alamy Stock Photo; 43 center left: WENN Ltd/Alamy Stock Photo; 43 bottom left: WENN Ltd/Alamy Stock Photo; 43 bottom center: dpa picture alliance/Alamy Stock Photo; 43 bottom right: snapshot/Future Image/Bedrosian/SZ Photo/The Image Works; 44 top left: Tom Bean/ Alamy Stock Photo; 44 bottom left: Bill Barksdale/Design Pics/Getty Images; 44 bottom right: Jodie Coston/Exactostock-1598/Superstock, Inc.; 45 top: BG Motorsports/Alamy Stock Photo; 45 center: Education Images/Getty Images; 45 bottom: The Granger Collection.

Maps by Map Hero, Inc.

Scholastic Inc., 557 Broadway, New York, NY 10012

1 2 3 4 5 6 7 8 9 10 R 28 27 26 25 24 23 22 21 20 19

**Front cover: John Ford's Point in
Monument Valley**

**Back cover: Rodeo event at the
Navajo Nation Fair**

Welcome to Arizona

Find the Truth!

Everything you are about to read is true **except** for one of the sentences on this page.

Which one is **TRUE**?

T or F Arizona was the 50th state to be admitted to the Union.

T or F Spanish explorers were the first Europeans to visit what is now Arizona.

Find the answers in this book.

UNITED STATES

Arizona

Contents

Map: This Is Arizona! **6**

1 Land and Wildlife

What is the terrain of Arizona like and
which plants and animals live there? **9**

2 Government

What are the different parts
of Arizona's government? **17**

THE BIG TRUTH!

Two-tailed
swallowtail

What Represents Arizona?

Which designs, objects,
plants, and animals
symbolize Arizona? **22**

Bolo tie

4

Horseshoe Bend

3 History

How did Arizona become
the state it is today? **25**

4 Culture

What do Arizonans do for work and fun? **35**

Famous People **42**

Did You Know That **44**

Resources **46**

Important Words **47**

Index **48**

About the Author **48**

Cactus wren

This Is Arizona!

COLORADO

NEVADA

Pipe Spring National Monument

Lake Powell

Grand Canyon

Colorado

Grand Canyon National Park

Colorado Plateau

Lake Mead

Sunset Crater Volcano National Monument

1 Petrified Forest National Park

Mohave Museum of History and Arts

KINGMAN

Route 66 Museum

Little Colorado

FLAGSTAFF

SEDONA

Verde

Mogollon Rim

LAKE HAVASU CITY

CALIFORNIA

ARIZONA

NEW MEXICO

Havasu National Wildlife Refuge

2 Heard Museum

Salt

PHOENIX

Colorado

Wildlife World Zoo

MESA

Arizona State Capitol

White Mountains

3

Gila

Gila

YUMA

Sonoran Desert

Tucson Children's Museum

San Pedro

Saguaro National Park

TUCSON

4

Kitt Peak National Observatory

Boothill Graveyard

NOGALES

MEXICO

0   50
Miles

1 Petrified Forest National Park

Despite its name, this park in northeastern Arizona is not a forest. It's actually a wide-open, rocky area covered in shrubs and grasses. Its name comes from the large number of tree **fossils** found there.

2 Heard Museum

Since 1929, this museum in Phoenix has displayed artwork by Native Americans. You'll see traditional art such as beadwork and baskets, as well as modern paintings and sculptures.

3 Wildlife World Zoo

Arizona's biggest zoo has everything from king vultures (pictured) to an extremely rare white alligator. It also has an aquarium with sea lions, sharks, and more.

4 Saguaro National Park

People come from all around to see the enormous saguaro cacti that give this park its name. The oldest cacti, more than 200 years old, are up to 75 feet (23 meters) tall!

Monument Valley, a 92,000-acre (37,231-hectare) park owned by the Navajo Nation, lies along Arizona's northern border with Utah.

CHAPTER 1

Land and Wildlife

Arizona is famous for its dramatic landscapes. Powerful rivers run between the striped red walls of deep canyons. Lush, green forests stretch along the sides of towering, snowcapped mountains. Spiky cacti sprout from the sandy sprawl of the state's many desert areas. With so many amazing things to explore, it's no wonder Arizona is such a popular place to live and visit.

Geography

Arizona is located in the middle of the U.S. Southwest. This large state can be divided into three basic regions. Southwestern Arizona is made up of low, dry desert. East of that is the Basin and Range region. Here, small, forested mountain ranges overlook desert landscapes below. Northern Arizona is covered by the Colorado Plateau. This rocky area has everything from tall mountains to deep canyons.

This map shows where the higher (red) and lower (green) areas are in Arizona.

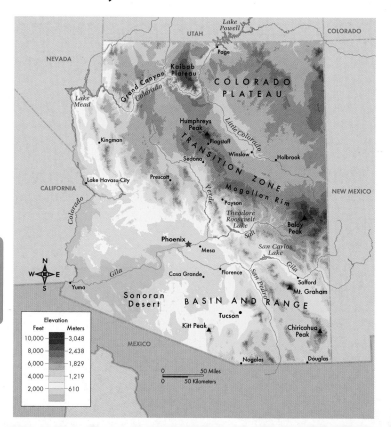

The Grand Canyon

The Grand Canyon is one of the world's most famous landmarks. Located in northwestern Arizona, its striped walls stretch 277 miles (446 kilometers) on either side of the Colorado River. At its widest point, the canyon measures 18 miles (29 km) across. At its deepest, the canyon's walls tower 1 mile (1.6 km) above the river. In 2016, more than six million people visited Grand Canyon National Park to witness its majestic scenery in person.

The Grand Canyon was declared a U.S. National Park in 1919.

Horseshoe Bend, a U-shaped bend in the Colorado River, is located near the town of Page.

Although Arizona is famous for its deserts, the state is also home to several large rivers, including the mighty Colorado. These waterways have played a major role in shaping the state's remarkable landscape. Over millions of years, the movement of their waters has cut through rocky surfaces. This has formed the state's canyons, **ravines,** and other distinctive features.

Climate

Arizona's summers are hot and dry, with temperatures often rising above 100 degrees Fahrenheit (37.8 degrees Celsius). But during the winter, temperatures can drop below freezing at night.

Little rain falls on average. But when it does rain, huge floods can form because the dry desert soil cannot absorb the water fast enough.

In dry areas such as the badlands of Petrified Forest National Park, there is so little rain that the ground begins to dry out and crack.

maximum TEMPERATURE 128°F   minimum TEMPERATURE -40°F

What Grows in Arizona?

More than 3,300 plant species grow throughout Arizona. In desert areas, cacti, shrubs, and grasses are most common. These types of plants grow very well in areas with limited water. Many of them produce beautiful flowers in spring, turning the desert landscape into a colorful canvas. On the sides of mountains, where water is more plentiful, a variety of trees grow. Many of them, such as pines, spruces, and junipers, stay green all year.

Coconino National Forest, near Flagstaff, is filled with green hills, mountains, and evergreen trees.

The Gila monster, which is found in Arizona's desert areas, is one of only two lizard species in the world to have a venomous bite.

Animals Everywhere

Many animals live in Arizona. Mountain lions and wolves stalk the wilderness in search of deer and other prey. Squirrels, rabbits, and foxes fill the state's forests, while bighorn sheep tiptoe along rocky cliffs. Hardy animals such as desert tortoises, Gila monsters, and scorpions can survive in even the hottest, driest parts of the state. Arizona is also home to many fascinating birds, from the gigantic California condor to tiny hummingbirds.

Since 1974, the Arizona State Capitol has served mainly as a museum and library, while government business is conducted in separate buildings nearby.

CHAPTER 2

Government

When Arizona became a U.S. **territory** in 1863, its capital was a city called Prescott. In the following years, the capital changed places frequently. First it moved to Tucson in 1867, then back to Prescott in 1877. Finally, in 1889, it settled in Phoenix. Since then, Phoenix has remained the center of government activity in Arizona. It has also grown to become the state's largest city, with more than 1.6 million residents.

The Three Branches

Arizona's state government is divided into three branches. Each has its own set of powers and responsibilities. Led by the governor, the executive branch carries out state laws. The legislative branch consists of a 30-member Senate and a 60-member House of Representatives. It writes and passes new state laws. Finally, the judicial branch is made up of the state's court system. It is in charge of interpreting state laws.

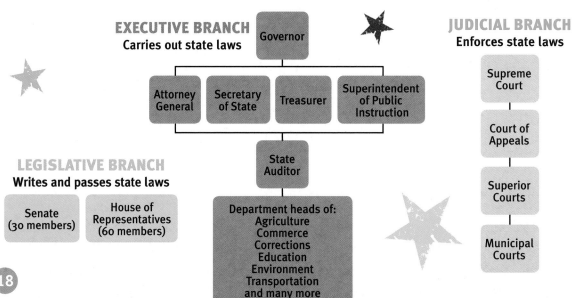

ARIZONA'S STATE GOVERNMENT

EXECUTIVE BRANCH
Carries out state laws

Governor

Attorney General | Secretary of State | Treasurer | Superintendent of Public Instruction

State Auditor

Department heads of:
Agriculture
Commerce
Corrections
Education
Environment
Transportation
and many more

JUDICIAL BRANCH
Enforces state laws

Supreme Court

Court of Appeals

Superior Courts

Municipal Courts

LEGISLATIVE BRANCH
Writes and passes state laws

Senate (30 members) | House of Representatives (60 members)

The town of Window Rock serves as the Navajo Nation's capital.

Native American Government

Arizona's Native American groups, such as the Navajo Nation and the Tohono O'odham Nation, have governments of their own. On **reservations**, people follow local laws just as they would follow state laws elsewhere. Native American governments also oversee services such as schools, fire departments, and police on the reservations. Each group has its own unique government and law enforcement. Many groups incorporate traditions that their people have followed for hundreds of years.

Arizona in the National Government

Each state elects officials to represent it in the U.S. Congress. Like every state, Arizona has two senators. The U.S. House of Representatives relies on a state's population to determine its numbers. Arizona has nine representatives in the House.

Every four years, states vote on the next U.S. president. Each state is granted a number of electoral votes based on its number of members in Congress. With two senators and nine representatives, Arizona has 11 electoral votes.

2 senators and 9 representatives

11 electoral votes

With eleven electoral votes, Arizona's voice in presidential elections is average compared to other states.

The People of Arizona

Elected officials in Arizona represent a population with a range of interests, lifestyles, and backgrounds.

Ethnicity (2016 estimates)

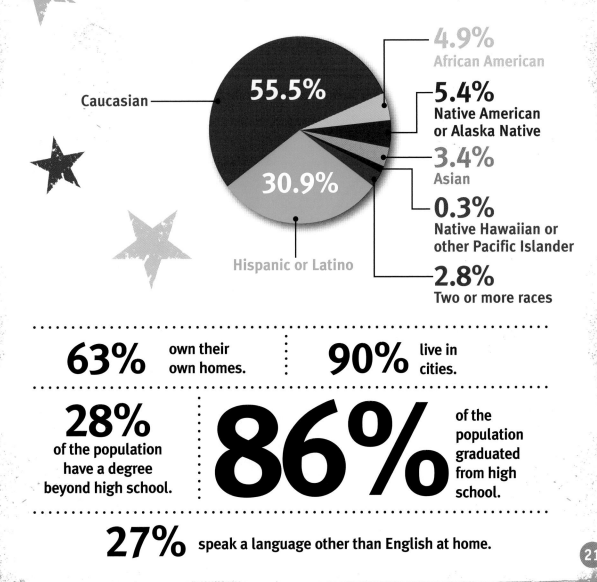

Caucasian — **55.5%**

30.9%
Hispanic or Latino

4.9%
African American

5.4%
Native American
or Alaska Native

3.4%
Asian

0.3%
Native Hawaiian or
other Pacific Islander

2.8%
Two or more races

63% own their own homes.

90% live in cities.

28% of the population have a degree beyond high school.

86% of the population graduated from high school.

27% speak a language other than English at home.

What Represents Arizona?

States choose specific animals, plants, and objects to represent the values and characteristics of the land and its people. Find out why these symbols were chosen to represent Arizona or discover surprising curiosities about them.

Seal

The state seal depicts many of the things Arizona was known for at the time it became a state, including a farm, a dam, a cattle ranch, and a mine.

Flag

The 13 red and yellow stripes on the Arizona flag represent the original 13 U.S. states. These colors are the same as those used on the national flag of Spain. This is a symbol of Arizona's time under Spanish rule.

Ringtail

STATE MAMMAL

Often mistaken for a cat, this mammal is actually a close relative of the raccoon.

Cactus Wren

STATE BIRD

This bird is named for its habit of making its nest inside spiky desert cacti.

Turquoise

STATE GEM

This blue gemstone is a common feature in traditional Native American jewelry in the Southwest.

Bolo Tie

STATE NECKWEAR

Popular in the Southwest, this tie features a metal piece that slides up and down a braided rope.

Two-tailed Swallowtail

STATE BUTTERFLY

One of the largest butterfly species in the country, this insect has a wingspan that can measure up to 5.5 inches (14 centimeters) across.

Copper

STATE METAL

Arizona produces more copper than any other state.

Wupatki National Monument in northern Arizona contains many Pueblo ruins.

CHAPTER 3

History

Even though Arizona is one of the country's youngest states, it has a very long history. People first arrived in the area about 12,000 years ago. Over time, the descendants of these early Arizonans settled down and formed the Mogollon, Hohokam, and Ancestral Pueblo cultures. No one knows why, but all three groups abandoned their settlements by the mid-1400s. Since then, many other people have called Arizona home.

Arizona's Native Americans

Around the time the original Arizonans were disappearing from the area, new people began arriving from the north. As these people settled in their new home, they developed into groups such as the Navajo and Apache. Because they came from the same group of people, the Navajo and Apache spoke similar languages. However, their lifestyles were very different. The Navajo mostly settled down and became farmers, while the Apache traveled often and relied on hunting for food.

This map shows where some of the major tribes lived in what is now Arizona before Europeans came.

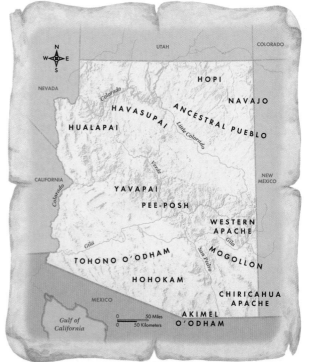

The Hopi are descendants of the Ancestral Pueblo people. Like their ancestors, they build elaborate, multistory buildings from stone and dried mud.

Arizona's other Native American groups include the Tohono O'odham, the Havasupais, and

Today, the Hopi and other Native American groups in Arizona continue the traditions their families have passed down for many generations.

the Hualapais. All of these peoples and others continue to make their homes in the state today. However, their ways of life were changed forever when a new group of settlers arrived in the 1500s.

Spanish Settlers

In 1539 and 1540, Spanish explorers came to Arizona chasing rumors of gold in the area. When they failed to find any gold, they left the area for more than 40 years. Upon returning in the 1580s, they discovered silver and other valuable metals. They began forming settlements, and more Spaniards arrived. Some of them hoped to become rich from Arizona's resources. Others founded **missions** and tried to convert Native Americans to Christianity.

This map shows routes Spaniards took as they explored and settled what is now Arizona.

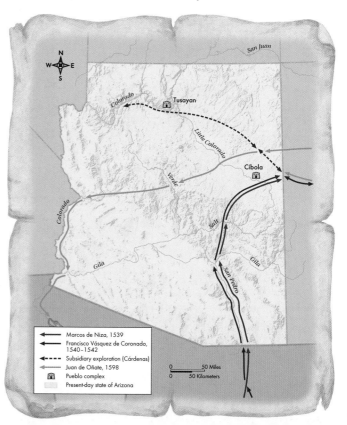

At Tumacácori National Historical Park in southern Arizona, visitors can explore the ruins of Spanish missions built hundreds of years ago.

The Spanish brought European diseases such as measles and chicken pox to Arizona. Because they had never encountered these illnesses before, the Native Americans had no **immunity** to them. When a Native American caught one of the diseases, it could quickly spread and kill everyone in a village. Sickness wasn't the only problem the Spaniards brought. Many Spanish settlers enslaved Native Americans and forced them to work in mines.

Changing Hands

Arizona began the 1800s as a Spanish territory. The land came under Mexican control in 1821 when Mexico won independence from Spain. In 1846, Mexico went to war with the United States over land in Texas. Two years later, the United States won. As part of the **treaty** that ended the war, the United States gained Texas and surrounding areas, including much of Arizona.

Timeline of Arizona Events

10,000 BCE
People arrive for the first time in what is now Arizona. Native American cultures begin developing in the area.

1848
The United States takes over part of Arizona after the Mexican-American War.

10,000 BCE	1539–1540 CE	1848	1853

1539–1540 CE
Spanish explorers arrive in Arizona looking for gold.

1853
The rest of present-day Arizona becomes U.S. property as part of the Gadsden Purchase.

The Wild West

In 1853, the United States purchased the rest of what is now Arizona from Mexico. Ten years later, Arizona was officially established as a U.S. territory. American settlers began pouring into Arizona in search of land and wealth. Small mining camps grew into bustling towns. Arizona was part of the Wild West, where there were few laws and gunfights could break out between outlaws and town marshals.

February 14, 1912
Arizona becomes the 48th U.S. state.

2010
Arizona draws national attention for its strict immigration laws.

1860–1870s | 1912 | 1942–1945 | 2010

1860–1870s
Native Americans battle the U.S. military in resistance to white settlement of their homeland.

1942–1945
Arizona is home to Japanese American internment camps during World War II.

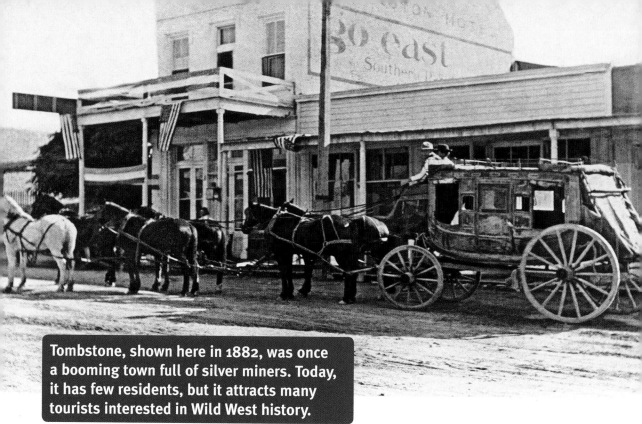

Tombstone, shown here in 1882, was once a booming town full of silver miners. Today, it has few residents, but it attracts many tourists interested in Wild West history.

Arizona in the 20th Century

By the beginning of the 1900s, the Wild West era was winding down. Arizona was home to more than 120,000 people, and the state was growing quickly. Many residents wanted their home territory to be a state, giving them a stronger voice in the national government. Finally, on February 14, 1912, Arizona became the 48th state.

Creating a New Path

Sandra Day O'Connor (1930–) grew up on an Arizona cattle ranch. After she became a lawyer, many Arizona law firms refused to hire her because she was a woman. Once she finally landed a job, she quickly began climbing the state's political ladder. From 1969 to 1975, she served as a state senator. She then worked as a judge. In 1981, O'Connor became the first female U.S. Supreme Court justice.

The Navajo are famous for weaving blankets and clothing with colorful, complex patterns.

CHAPTER **4**

Culture

Today, Arizona continues to grow at a rapid pace. People from all over are drawn by its warm weather and scenic landscape. Big cities such as Phoenix and Tucson are cultural centers of the Southwest. They are packed with museums, theaters, restaurants, and much more. Throughout Arizona, Native American, Spanish, and Mexican traditions blend with influences from the many other people who have settled in the state over the years. This gives Arizona its unique character.

Fun and Games

Sports are a big deal for many Arizonans. In Phoenix, professional teams represent the state in several sports. Basketball fans root for the Phoenix Suns and Phoenix Mercury. Those who like football cheer on the Arizona Cardinals. Hockey lovers watch the Arizona Coyotes play. Baseball fans follow the Arizona Diamondbacks. There are also many college teams, including the Arizona State University Sun Devils and the University of Arizona Wildcats.

The Phoenix Mercury was one of the original eight teams in the Women's National Basketball Association when the league was formed in 1996.

Steer wrestling is one of several rodeo events held each year at La Fiesta de los Vaqueros in Tucson.

Fine Festivities

Almost every town or city in Arizona is home to a number of yearly celebrations. Some of these events draw huge crowds from all over, while others are enjoyed mainly by local people. Arizona hosts some of the country's biggest, most exciting **rodeos**, including Prescott's Frontier Days and Tucson's La Fiesta de los Vaqueros (Spanish for "Festival of Cowboys"). Other festivals celebrate everything from Native American culture to Arizona's Wild West history.

Workers in Arizona pick lettuce and place it onto the conveyor belt of a harvesting machine.

Arizonans at Work

Agriculture and mining drew thousands of people to Arizona in the 1800s. These industries remain an important part of the state's economy today. Arizona's farmers grow everything from lettuce and citrus fruit to cotton and hay. Ranchers raise cattle, pigs, and other livestock. The state's mines produce a huge amount of copper, as well as other metals and some gemstones. Arizona's factories turn these and other raw materials into goods such as clothing, electronics, and furniture. Many of the state's people also work in the tourism industry.

Growing Industries

Many new jobs in Arizona will come from the tech world. Giant companies such as Apple and Intel have facilities in Arizona, providing jobs for many of those who have moved to the state in recent years.

Aerospace and defense companies are also a big part of Arizona's job market. At these companies, Arizona workers help create everything from airplanes to missiles.

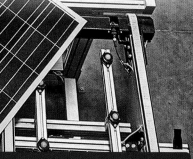

Workers build solar panels that capture energy from sunlight at a factory in Goodyear.

39

Time to Eat!

Mexican influences are everywhere when it comes to Arizona's local cuisine. Restaurants and home cooks alike love to serve up salsa, tacos, enchiladas, and other classic Mexican dishes. They also cook with fruits and vegetables that are native to the Southwest, including spicy chili peppers, sweet cactus fruit, and tangy green **tomatillos**.

Pico de Gallo

Ask an adult to help you!

Try this simple, refreshing salsa with tortilla chips or as a topping for tacos.

Ingredients
1 1/2 cups diced tomatoes
1/2 teaspoon salt, plus more to taste
1/3 cup finely chopped cilantro
1/4 cup finely chopped white onion
1 finely chopped jalapeño pepper
Juice of 1/2 lime

Directions
Place the tomatoes in a strainer over a bowl or sink. Add the salt and toss to combine. Allow the salted tomatoes to drain for about 20 minutes. This gets rid of extra water in the tomatoes. When they are ready, combine the tomatoes with the rest of the ingredients in a bowl and toss everything together. Add salt to taste.

Many visitors to the Grand Canyon enjoy rafting trips along the Colorado River.

An Incredible State

From the wide-open spaces of the state's biggest deserts to the busy city streets of downtown Phoenix, there is always something to see or do in Arizona. It is no surprise that it has long been one of the nation's fastest-growing states. People love Arizona's abundant sunshine, unique culture, and breathtaking scenery. It is truly one of the jewels of the American Southwest. ★

Famous People

Cochise

(?–1874) was an Apache chief who helped lead a resistance movement against U.S. efforts to take over Arizona and the surrounding area. Today, one of Arizona's counties is named after him.

Cesar Chavez

(1927–1993) was a labor leader who fought for the rights of farmworkers. He was born and raised in Yuma.

Charles Mingus

(1922–1979) was a highly influential jazz bassist and pianist. He was born in Nogales.

Reggie Jackson

(1946–) is a legendary baseball player who earned the nickname "Mr. October" for his amazing batting during the Major League Baseball playoffs, which take place in October. He attended college at Arizona State University in Tempe.

Ted Danson

(1947–) is an award-winning actor who has appeared in many movies and TV shows, including *Cheers* and *CSI*. He grew up in Flagstaff.

Stevie Nicks

(1948–) is a singer-songwriter who came to fame as a member of Fleetwood Mac. She later had a successful solo career. She is from Phoenix.

Michael Biehn

(1956–) is an actor who has starred in films such as *The Terminator*, *Aliens*, and *The Abyss*. He was born in Anniston.

Kerri Strug

(1977–) is a gymnast who won an Olympic gold medal in 1996. She is from Tucson.

Emma Stone

(1988–) is an Academy Award–winning actress who has starred in such films as *La La Land* and *Birdman*. She grew up in Scottsdale.

Danielle Fishel

(1981–) is an actress best known for her role in the TV series *Boy Meets World* and *Girl Meets World*. She is from Mesa.

Michelle Branch

(1983–) is a Grammy Award–winning singer-songwriter. She is from Sedona.

Did You Know That ...

The Navajo Nation has the country's largest Native American reservation. It covers more than 27,000 square miles (69,930 sq km) across three states: Arizona, Utah, and New Mexico.

Arizonans like to give their spicy homemade salsa fun names. Some local varieties include "Attack of the Fire-Breathing Tomatoes" and "Heartburn Hotel."

Enough cotton is grown in Arizona each year to create a pair of jeans for every person in the country.

Arizona is a very popular tourist destination. More than 44 million people visit the state each year. About half of all visitors spend time in the Phoenix area, where they enjoy attractions and events such as NASCAR races at ISM Raceway.

Arizona has 24 national parks and monuments, including Casa Grande Ruins National Monument (pictured). That's more than any other state except California.

Did you find the truth?

(**F**) Arizona was the 50th state to be admitted to the Union.

(**T**) Spanish explorers were the first Europeans to visit what is now Arizona.

Resources

Books

Cunningham, Kevin, and Peter Benoit. *The Navajo.* New York: Children's Press, 2011.

Gregory, Josh. *Cesar Chavez.* New York: Children's Press, 2015.

Gregory, Josh. *Grand Canyon.* New York: Children's Press, 2017.

Rozett, Louise (ed.). *Fast Facts About the 50 States: Plus Puerto Rico and Washington, D.C.* New York: Children's Press, 2010.

Somervill, Barbara A. *Arizona.* New York: Children's Press, 2015.

Visit this Scholastic website for more information on Arizona:

★ www.factsfornow.scholastic.com
Enter the keyword **Arizona**

Important Words

aerospace (AIR-oh-spase) of or having to do with the science and technology of jet flight or space travel

fossils (FAH-suhlz) bones, shells, or other traces of an animal or plant from millions of years ago, preserved as rock

immunity (i-MYOON-i-tee) natural resistance to a disease

missions (MISH-uhnz) churches or other places where people sent to a foreign country to teach about religion live and work

ravines (ruh-VEENS) steep, extremely narrow valleys

reservations (rez-ur-VAY-shuhnz) areas of land set aside by the government for a special purpose, particularly land that belongs to Native American groups

rodeos (ROH-dee-ohz) contests in which cowboys and cowgirls compete at riding wild horses and bulls and catching cattle with lassos

territory (TER-ih-tor-ee) an area officially connected with or owned by a country that is outside the country's main borders

tomatillos (toh-muh-TEE-yohz) small green or greenish-purple fruit related to tomatoes

treaty (TREE-tee) a formal written agreement between two or more countries

Index

Page numbers in **bold** indicate illustrations.

animals, **7**, **15**, **23**, **37**, 38
art, **7**

Basin and Range region, 10
birds, **7**, 15, **23**

cacti, **7**, 9, 14, **23**, 40
Casa Grande Ruins National
    Monument, **45**
climate, **13**, 35
Coconino National Forest, **14**
Colorado Plateau, 10
Colorado River, **11**, **12**, **41**

deserts, **8–9**, 10, **13**, 14, **15**, 23
diseases, 29

education, 19, 21
elevation, **10**
explorers, **28**, **30**

famous people, **42–43**
farming, 22, 26, 38, **42**, **44**
festivals, **37**
food, 26, 38, **40**, **44**

Gadsden Purchase, 30
Gila monsters, **15**

Grand Canyon, **11**, **41**

Heard Museum, **7**

immigration, **31**
internment camps, **31**

jobs, 38, **39**

land, **8–9**, **10**, **11**, **12**, **14**
languages, 21, 26

maps, **6**, **10**, **26**, **28**
Mexican-American War, **30**
mining, 29, 31, **32**, 38
missions, 28, **29**
Monument Valley, **8–9**
mountains, 10, **14**
music, **42**, **43**

national government, 20, 32, **33**
Native Americans, 7, **8–9**, **19**, 21,
    23, **24–25**, **26–27**, 28, 29, 30,
    31, **34–35**, 37, 42, **44**

O'Connor, Sandra Day, **33**

Petrified Forest National Park, **7**, 13

Phoenix, **7**, **16–17**, 35, 36, 43, **45**
plants, **7**, **14**, **38**, 40, **44**

reservations, 19, 44
rivers, **11**, **12**, **41**
rodeos, **37**

Saguaro National Park, **7**
settlers, **24–25**, 26, 27, **28–29**,
    31, 35
sports, 36, **42**, **43**, **45**
state capital, **16–17**
state government, **16–17**, 18
statehood, 31, 32
state symbols, **22–23**

timeline, **30–31**
Tombstone, **32**
tourism, **32**, 38, 45
Tucson, 17, 35, **37**, 43
Tumacácori National Historical
    Park, **29**

wildflowers, 14
Wildlife World Zoo, **7**
Wild West, 31, **32**, 37
Wupatki National Monument,
    24–25

About the Author

Josh Gregory is the author of more than 120 books for young readers. He currently lives in Chicago, Illinois. He would love to see the Grand Canyon in person someday!